MRS
BEETON
FISH &
SEAFOOD

Mrs Beeton How to Cook

Mrs Beeton Soups & Sides

Mrs Beeton Fish & Seafood

Mrs Beeton Chicken, Other Birds & Game

Mrs Beeton Classic Meat Dishes

Mrs Beeton Cakes & Bakes

Mrs Beeton Puddings

MRS BEETON
FISH & SEAFOOD

ISABELLA BEETON
& GERARD BAKER

FOREWORD BY MARK HIX

For my grandmothers Nora Baker and Elsie Hinch,
who spanned the gap between Isabella and me.

Gerard Baker

This edition published in Great Britain in 2012 by Weidenfeld & Nicolson
Originally published in 2011 by Weidenfeld & Nicolson as part of *Mrs Beeton How to Cook*

1 3 5 7 9 10 8 6 4 2

Design & Art Direction by Julyan Bayes
Photography by Andrew Hayes-Watkins
Illustration by Bold & Noble. Additional illustration by Carol Kearns
Food Styling by Sammy-Jo Squire
Prop Styling by Giuliana Casarotti
Edited by Zelda Turner

A CIP catalogue record for this book is available from the British Library.
ISBN 978 0 297 86686 2

The Orion Publishing Group's policy is to use papers that are natural, renewable and recyclable
products and made from wood grown in sustainable forests. The logging and manufacturing
processes are expected to conform to the environmental regulations of the country of origin.

Printed and bound in Spain

Weidenfeld & Nicolson
The Orion Publishing Group Ltd
Orion House
5 Upper St Martin's Lane
London WC2H 9EA

An Hachette UK Company

www.orionbooks.co.uk

CONTENTS

FOREWORD

Just when it seems that Mrs Beeton is out of date, she is reincarnated. And suddenly we are all interested in looking at her work again ...

I have lots of rare tattered antique editions of Mrs Beeton in amongst the thousand or so cookbooks that crowd my shelves. Even so, the volume that sits on my kitchen table today – the book you are holding in your hands right now – feels like something fresh. By which I mean it is full of dishes that seem so current they wouldn't look out of place in one of my own restaurants, or any kitchen serving modern British food.

Fish should be treated with respect. We cannot afford to be cavalier about the fish we catch, or the seafood we buy to cook, as some species are not as plentiful today as in Mrs Beeton's time. Having been brought up by the sea and now escaping back to the coast most weekends to keep an eye on my fish restaurant – always squeezing in as much fishing as I can – I feel attached to the sea and what it produces for the table.

Mrs Beeton shows us how to get the most out of our fish. Using techniques such as potting and cocottes, she makes a little go a long way. Many of these methods are forgotten today, but they should be revisited by anyone interested in new tastes and spending less. Economically, they make perfect sense.

In this book, you will find reminders of lovely old classics, dishes that feel perfect for a dinner party, and wholesome family dinners. The approach throughout is simple and respectful. Which means, for anyone wanting to prepare and cook good food, Mrs Beeton is still very much alive.

Mark Hix

THE INIMITABLE MRS BEETON

When Isabella Beeton first published *Beeton's Book of Household Management* in 1861, Britain was changing from a rural society, in which large numbers of people were involved in farming and many grew their own fruit and vegetables at home, to an industrialised one, where the development of modern transport networks, refrigeration and kitchen appliances brought a world of food to our fingertips.

Today, most of us have an image of Mrs Beeton as a matronly figure – brisk, efficient and experienced in the kitchen. In fact, Isabella Beeton was young and recently married, juggling working outside the home with running her household and coping with the demands of a husband and young family. Having worked on it throughout her early twenties, she saw her book published at the age of 25 and died just three years later.

Although she wrote of housekeepers, butlers and valets, her semi-detached in Hatch End was a world away from the big country houses of the preceding century, and although it is likely that she had some help in the kitchen, she almost certainly managed her home and most of the cooking herself. Her book was inspired by an awareness of the challenges faced by women like herself – and with that in mind, she used her position as editor of *The Englishwoman's Domestic Magazine* to pull together the best recipes and advice from a wide range of sources.

She was among the first revolutionary food writers to style recipes in the format that we are familiar with today, setting out clear lists of ingredients and details of time taken, average cost and portions produced (this last being entirely her invention). She also offered notes on how to source the best food for her recipes – placing particular emphasis on such old-fashioned (or, in our eyes, surprisingly modern) ideas as the use of seasonal, local produce and the importance of animal welfare.

It is easy to see why Mrs Beeton's core themes – buy well, cook well and eat well – are as relevant today as they were 150 years ago. Her original book was written with an awareness of household economy that we can take lessons from too. Because we have access to so much so easily, we often forget to consider how to get the most out of each ingredient – yet maximising flavour and nutrient value and minimising waste is as relevant in the twenty-first century as it was in 1861.

The right ingredients

Mrs Beeton's original recipes have needed careful adaptation. In some cases, the modern recipes are amalgamations of more than one Beeton recipe or suggestion, which I hope give a more coherent whole. Many of the ingredients that may seem at first glance universal are so different today from those varieties Isabella would have been familiar with that using them in the original way can

give quite different results to those intended. For those reasons, quantities needed to be not only converted but checked and altered. And all those cases where Mrs Beeton advised adding salt or sugar or honey or spices 'to taste' have been pinned down in real quantities, always keeping in mind both flavour and authenticity.

In the case of many of the meat and fish dishes in particular, the modern recipes are amalgamations of more than one Beeton recipe or suggestion. Where a Victorian cook would have happily chosen a plain fish from one chapter and a sauce from another, we tend to prefer the convenience of having everything in one place.

Cooking methods, too, were in some cases not replicable and in others simply no longer the best way of achieving the desired results. A significant factor in this is that the domestic oven was in its infancy in 1861, and Mrs Beeton was not able to make full use of it in her book. Most kitchens would instead have been equipped with old-fashioned ranges, and there is much mention of setting things before the fire, turning and basting. Roasting meat, which we now consider a simple process, required constant attention 150 years ago. Oven temperatures, therefore, have all had to be deduced from a mixture of reading between the lines, comparing modern recipes, and testing, testing, testing.

The end result, however, has been to produce dishes that Mrs Beeton would, hopefully, have been happy to call her own.

The legacy

After Isabella Beeton died early in 1865, her book took on a life of its own. It was endlessly enlarged, modern recipes were added and eventually, in the many, many editions of the book that have been published in the past 150 years, the spirit of the original was lost.

The picture of British food that Isabella painted in the first edition was about to change wholesale, and her book was destined to change with it. The aim of this collection is to reverse those changes: to return to real, wholesome, traditional British food, which Mrs Beeton might be proud to recognise as her own – and to put to rest the matronly image.

'Nothing can be of greater consequence to a cook than to have the fish good; as if this important course in a dinner does not give satisfaction, it is rarely that the repast goes off well.'

Beeton's Book of Household Management

INTRODUCTION

The British are remarkably unadventurous with fish, choosing to consume a very limited range of species even though there are many others available. This has led to over-consumption of the most popular species, and the stocks of some fish – notably cod and skate – have become scarce in our native waters.

Looking back at recipes from 150 years ago the decline of these species is clear to see. Mrs Beeton's recipe for a cod head and shoulders feeds six to eight people, which shows that much larger fish than we are ever likely to find in our home markets were available to her. Even at that time steam-powered boats were able to bring in ever-greater quantities of fish from further and further beyond their traditional grounds, and Mrs Beeton marvelled at how it would seem impossible that the cod population could survive such intense fishing – we now know that it could not.

The good news is that delicious alternatives are available. While it is possible to buy, for example, cod that has been caught in other waters and frozen at sea, there are plenty of excellent substitutes, such as coley and pollock, which you can buy fresh. There is every reason to go against the national tendency, be adventurous and try something different.

The other big change over time in terms of the fish we eat is that freshwater fish were far more prevalent up to industrialisation, and available for people to eat. At the time Mrs Beeton was writing, ponds were still maintained containing a variety of species to provide food for large houses – among them brown trout, eels, pike and many others. Native brown trout are still commonly available, but the eel population, sadly, has reduced hugely because of poor habitat management. Freshwater fish are truly delicious – the best way to enjoy them is simply grilled with butter and lemon. However, catching and smoking them over a peat fire is also an exceptional pleasure.

If you are interested in trying freshwater fish today you generally have to catch them yourself. Throughout England and Wales a licence, available from the Post Office, is required to fish for freshwater species in open rivers or closed ponds. If in doubt, you should contact the Environment Agency in England and Wales. In Scotland virtually all fishing rights are under private ownership, so you will require the permission of the landowner – contact the Scottish Environment Protection Agency for further information.

Sustainable fish and shellfish

When buying fish, as a priority, look for fish that have been caught sustainably because species will undoubtedly become extinct if stocks are not treated with respect. It is up to us all as consumers to exert financial pressure on suppliers by only buying sustainable fish. Check the label and look for the Marine Stewardship Council (MSC) mark. This international body offers certification for

sustainable fisheries, using a range of industry and scientific experts to verify independently that they operate in an ecologically sensitive manner. Small and large fisheries around the world are certified, and many shops and caterers will only use or stock MSC certified fish. The RSPCA also offers certification through its Freedom Food initiative. Contact details for these organisations are listed at the back of the book. Some species – all swordfish and shark species and all tuna apart from skipjack – are so threatened it is wrong to buy them under any circumstances. White fish that does not bear the MSC label should also be questioned, unless you are buying it straight off a day boat or from a shore-based fisherman.

In addition, there are some methods of harvesting and farming fish that threaten the wider ecosystem and disrupt local economies. Avoid any fish produced by the following methods:

* Prawns farmed in the Far East. This style of farming is destroying tropical mangroves.

* Scallops dredged in British coastal waters. The dredging process destroys the sea-floor habitat of many other species.

* Atlantic salmon badly and over-intensively farmed. Poorly managed salmon farms in the Atlantic have caused the spread of sea lice to wild salmon. Responsibly farmed salmon will carry an MSC or RSPCA mark.

Who is in control?

The local management of sea-fish resources is largely the responsibility of Inshore Fisheries and Conservation Authorities and the Marine Management Organisation, which have the power to control fishing, to establish marine reserves to protect marine resources and control all boats landing fish in UK waters. Although any boat landing fish in an EU port is subject to inspection, boats from other countries still continue to fish freely for severely threatened species such as tuna.

Fisheries that border failed states where there is no local management in place are particularly culpable. The national fisheries ministers agree European quotas annually in December, based loosely on scientific advice. Naturally, each country will try to get the most from the system it can to protect its traditional fishing rights, so the quotas set are usually well in excess of the amounts advised by scientists.

Due to the quota system, any boat catching fish (and other marine species such as whales and dolphin) other than those for which it has quota must discard those fish (known as bycatch) back to sea, even though they will be dead. This much-criticised system is hugely destructive to the marine environment. The prawn-netting industry has the largest bycatch of all with 5–10 tonnes of fish discarded for every tonne of prawns caught. This represents one-quarter of the world's wasted catch. It is hoped that reform of the Common Fisheries Policy, currently under review, will reform the way that the EU manages marine resources.

Storing fresh and frozen fish

Remove all packaging and place the fish or shellfish on a plate. Cover with a damp cloth and seal tightly with cling film. Shellfish may be stored for 3–4 days, but should be transferred to a clean dish regularly so it does not sit in any juice that drains from it. Before using, rinse it thoroughly in cold water. Fish should ideally be cooked within 1–2 days of purchase. However, fish you catch yourself needs to be chilled 12–24 hours before cooking to allow the flesh to set. This rule does not apply to hake or mackerel, which should only be eaten when very fresh. To freeze fish, wrap it tightly in cling film and then a layer of foil to prevent not only freezer burn but also flavour contamination to and from other things in the freezer. If you buy frozen fish and intend to use it immediately, let it defrost in the fridge first before you cook it.

Preparing Fish

When we talk of preparing fish, we tend to divide species into round and flat types because the two are treated differently. Coley, mackerel and whiting, among others, are considered round fish, while fish such as sole, plaice, flounder and halibut are known as flatfish.

Round fish

Scaling

This is a messy process, but not difficult. Take hold of the fish firmly by its tail, using a cloth to ensure you get a good grip, and scrape the blade of your knife along the fish from the tail end towards the head.

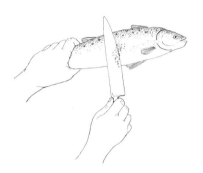

Repeat until all the scales have been removed – you can check by running your fingers along the fish from tail to head. If any scales remain they will feel sharp; if not, the skin will be soft and smooth.

Gutting

If you are going to cook the fish whole, you now need to gut it. Place the fish on its side on a board with its belly facing you. If you are right handed, the head should be to your right. Insert the point of your knife into the anal vent, which should be clearly visible near the tail. Cut from here towards the head, slicing the belly open, and stop once you have cut through the base of the gills, which will offer some resistance to the knife. Open up the fish and pull out the innards. They will be attached at the head end. If they don't pull away easily use your knife to cut them away and then scrape out the bloodline which runs along the spine of the fish, using your fingernail or the tip of your knife.

Next, remove the gills. Your earlier cut should have separated the two gills from one another at the fish's throat; if not, use a strong pair of scissors. Next, pull or cut the gills away from the fish's head. For bigger fish you may need a good pair of scissors or a sharp knife to help you with this. Finally, discard the gills, rinse the fish thoroughly under a cold tap and pat dry.

Filleting

Round fish are divided into two fillets, with one running along each side the backbone. It is easier to fillet a fish with the guts in place. Lay the fish on its side on a board with its back facing towards you and, if you are right-handed, its head on the left.

Grip the head firmly with your non-cutting hand, using a cloth to ensure it doesn't slip. Cut into the fish just behind the gills, as you would do if you wanted to cut off the fish's head, and slice down as far as the backbone.

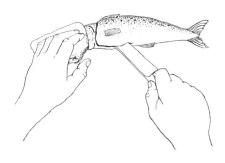

Next, slide the knife into your first cut, with the blade pointing towards the tail. Still holding the head firmly, make several short, horizontal cuts towards the tail, feeling for the backbone with your knife and cutting as close to it as possible. After the first few cuts you will be able to peel back the fillet, helping you to see more clearly. Continue cutting until you reach the tail.

Now flip the fish over and cut away the other fillet in exactly the same way as you did the first one. Do not at any point cut towards your hand, as the knife can easily slip and injure you.

Once you have filleted the fish, pluck out any small bones left behind with a pair of tweezers or small pliers, then rinse the fillets under a cold tap and pat dry.

Skinning

You can remove the skin from fish fillets by placing them skin-side down on a board and sliding a sharp knife in between flesh and skin. Start at the tail end and slice towards the head. If you are right-handed, place the fish with its head to your right and press down on the skin firmly at the tail end with your left hand. Next insert the knife, angling it towards the head end and very slightly downwards. With a sharp knife and a little practice you will be able to slide it smoothly between skin and flesh – moving the knife from side to side in a gentle sawing motion may help.

Flatfish

Gutting

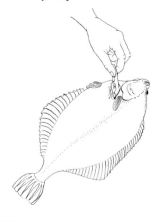

To gut a flatfish place it dark side up and locate the small pectoral fin just beyond the gills. Just beneath this (in the direction of the tail) is the belly. You should be able to feel the outline of the small, soft belly cavity, surrounded by firm flesh.

Using a small knife, cut a flap around the edge of the belly cavity large enough for you to reach in and remove its contents. Finally, rinse the fish under a cold tap and pat it dry.

Skinning

Dover sole in partcular are usually skinned before being cooked whole, on the bone – but this method works for other flatfish too. First, place the fish flat on a board, dark side up, and make a small, shallow slit across the tail. The idea is to cut through the skin but not the flesh.

Next, insert either your knife or your finger horizontally into the cut, pointing towards the head, and move it gently from side to side to separate the skin from the flesh. Now turn the fish so that the tail is facing away from you, grip the skin flap you have created and pull it sharply towards you. The skin should come off easily in one piece. It is not necessary to skin the underside of the fish.

Filleting

Flatfish have four fillets – two on the upper (dark-skinned) side of the fish and two on the underside. The fillets on the top of the fish are slightly larger. If you intend to skin the fish, do so before filleting, following the instructions above. Note that if a flatfish is very small it is best cooked whole, on the bone. Some flatfish, for example dabs, are best cooked whole whatever their size.

Start with the dark side of the fish facing up. First, cut a straight line down the middle of the fish from head to tail, cutting down until you feel the backbone resisting your knife. Next, insert the full length of your knife into the first cut and, using the bones to guide you, slide it into a horizontal position with the blade pointing outwards. It doesn't matter which side you fillet first, but right-handers will find it easier to start with the left fillet.

Now, with your knife pointing slightly downwards to stay as close as possible to the bones, make several short cuts out towards the side of the fish. Once you have started you will be able to peel back the flesh, making it easier to see what you are doing. Cut right to the edge to release the first fillet, then repeat the process on the opposite side. Once you have finished the first two fillets, turn the fish over and cut the fillets from the underside in the same way.

Preparing a crab

If you want to kill your own crab, take a long, thin screwdriver or strong skewer. Place the crab on a cloth on a board with its mouth towards you and set a bowl ready nearby. Hold the crab securely with a cloth and insert the screwdriver or skewer quickly and firmly into the crab between its eyes, then move the implement from left to right. Then, lift the small tail flap and insert the screwdriver or skewer firmly into the groove underneath. These two steps performed in quick succession will destroy the crab's nerve clusters, killing it as quickly and humanely as possible. Place the crab in the bowl to catch any juice it leaks.

Now put a large pan over a high heat and add 4 litres of water and 1½ teaspoons of salt. Cover and bring to a rapid boil. Lift the lid and add the crab, then replace the lid and cook for 12 minutes per kilogramme from the point at which the water comes back to a simmer. If you are cooking several smaller crabs, only cook two at a time in this volume of water. Just before the crab is cooked, take a large bowl and fill it three-quarters full with ice and water. When the crab is cooked, remove it carefully with a pair of tongs and plunge into the bowl of iced water. Leave for 30 minutes until absolutely cold, rinse briefly under cold running water, then drain and chill, covered, in the bowl. To prepare a cooked crab, follow the instructions on page 45.

Preparing a lobster

If you want to kill your own lobster, place the animal on a board in front of you. If you intend to poach it, have the pan ready, according to the instructions on page 54. Take a large knife. Look at the back of the lobster's head. You will notice a line running from its eyes down its back. About 3cm from the eyes there is another line crossing the head. Keeping the blade parallel to the long line, insert your knife at the point at which the lines cross, piercing through to the board beneath. The lobster will die quickly using this method, as you will have severed its main nerve cord. Now cook the lobster according to the recipe – see pages 54 and 62.

Preparing oysters

Put a clean tea towel over your hand and set an oyster into your palm. Hold the oyster knife in your other hand and carefully but firmly insert it into the hinge of the shell. Push hard and twist, and the shell should open.

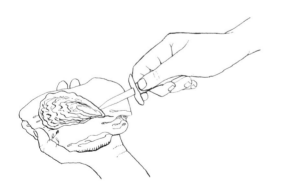
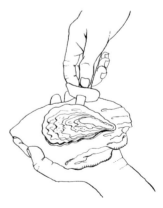

Cooking Techniques

Most fish flesh is delicate and only needs light cooking. It should, however, be cooked fully to 60°C to kill off any parasitic worms the fish may be carrying. If you intend to eat fish raw, for example as sushi, freezing it for a minimum of 1 week will also kill off any parasites.

Poaching
This is a gentle technique where fish are lightly cooked in court bouillon at around 80–90°C. This allows heat to penetrate gradually so that the outer layers do not overcook. After poaching, the fish is drained and served with a sauce.

Baking
This is a good method for cooking a whole fish, particularly salmon. The fish is delicately seasoned and sometimes stuffed, wrapped in a foil parcel and baked in a low to medium oven.

Roasting
This is a robust method of cooking that suits highly flavoured fish. This technique is used for small, whole fish or shellfish that can be cooked through quickly without the outer layers becoming overcooked. Roasting is suitable for herring, mackerel and scallops. Fish are roasted in a hot oven with fat, the intention being to brown the outside of the flesh.

Grilling
This versatile method can be used for cooking many kinds of fish, either as fillets or whole. Shellfish, such as half lobsters and oysters, can also be cooked under a grill.

Frying
Fish fillets, shellfish and small fish are suitable for frying either in oil or butter. The flesh develops a tasty brown crust and a delicious, savoury aroma. To protect it and add texture some fish benefit from being given a coating of oats or flour before frying.

A Seasonal Guide

Fish varies in quality depending on when it is harvested in relation to its life cycle. Fish that are preparing to spawn will have weak and soft flesh. This means most white fish are at their best in the winter months when they do not breed. What is and isn't sustainable is constantly being updated, but the Marine Conservation Society (MSC) has produced a handy table to enable you to avoid buying fish during their breeding or spawning times, and below the size at which they mature (see pages 24 and 25). Your local fishmonger will also be a good source of information on what's in season, where a fish comes from and how it was caught.

The cold waters of the UK provide an environment that enables shellfish to grow slowly and develop a rich deep flavour but, like fish, if they are harvested when they are spawning the flavour and texture will not be as good. Avoid buying fresh shellfish in the late spring and summer months. Local bylaws affect what types of shellfish you are legally allowed to collect. If you are in any doubt, contact your local authority for advice.

Britain's native oyster is protected from fishing during the summer breeding cycle, which is why it is illegal to fish for it during months without an 'r' in the name. Pacific oysters can be sold year-round because, in UK waters, they are mostly farmed.

A Note on Herbs

Fresh herbs are commonly used today to accompany fish, as they have been throughout our culinary history. Care must be taken, though, to use herbs so that they delicately balance the flavour of the fish that they are served with. Too much of any seasoning, and too high a cooking temperature, will mean that the flavour of your principal ingredient is dominated.

To use fresh herbs, the best option is to grow your own. This can easily be done on a kitchen windowsill as many herbs are available in seed form. An exception is tarragon, as the best, French form is only really available when taken from cuttings, but it can be bought widely as a plant from plant nurseries.

If you have a warm corner on your balcony or garden, most herbs can be grown out of doors in the summer. Only chervil, of all the fine herbs we use with fish, prefers cooler and damper conditions.

Spring

Borage, chervil, chives, coriander, dill, mint, parsley, rosemary, sorrel, thyme

Summer

Basil, borage, chervil, chives, coriander, dill, hyssop, mint, oregano, parsley, rosemary, sage, savoury, sorrel, tarragon, thyme

Autumn

Basil, chives, coriander, oregano, mint, parsley, rosemary, sage, sorrel, tarragon, thyme

Winter

Chives, mint, parsley, rosemary, sage, thyme

chervil

tarragon

sorrel

thyme

WHAT TO BUY

	January	February	March	April	May
Bib or poutin	●	●	●		●
Black sea bream or porgy	●	●	●		
Brown trout				●	●
Clam, carpet or venus shell	●	●	●	●	●
Clam, razor	●	●	●	●	
Cockle	●	●	●	●	●
Cod, Atlantic	●				●
Coley or saithe				●	●
Crab, brown or edible				●	●
Crab, spider	●	●	●		
Dab	●	●	●	●	●
Dover sole	●	●	●	●	●
Dublin Bay Prawn/langoustine	●	●	●	●	
Flounder	●	●	●		●
Grey gurnard	●	●	●		
Haddock	●	●	●	●	●
Hake, European				●	●
Herring or sild	●	●	●	●	●
Lemon sole	●	●	●	●	●
Lobster	●	●	●	●	●
Lythe or pollack					●
Mackerel	●	●	●	●	●
Mussel	●	●	●		
Pilchard (adult) or sardine	●	●	●		
Plaice				●	●
Northern or cold-water prawn	●	●	●	●	●
Red gurnard	●	●	●	●	●
Red mullet	●	●	●		
Scallop, King	●	●	●		
Scallop, Queen	●	●			
Seabass or bass	●	●	●		
Whelk	●	●	●	●	●

AND WHEN TO BUY IT

June	July	August	September	October	November	December

Buy fish   Avoid buying fish

SOMETHING
TO START

OYSTERS

Native oysters were once cheap and plentiful enough to use as a filler in fish pies and other recipes, where their flavour blended well with the other ingredients and their juices added body. The pollution caused by the Industrial Revolution put paid to this because oysters tend to accumulate toxic compounds in polluted waters. Today, the larger Pacific oyster is the most commonly available species because it is farmed widely. Native oysters can still be found, however, and are worth searching out. Although Mrs Beeton always cooked oysters, they are widely appreciated today served raw on the half shell. A modern serving suggestion of shallot vinegar is included with this selection of recipes.

GRILLED OYSTERS WITH DOUBLE CREAM

✳ Serves 4 ✳ Preparation time 15 minutes ✳ Cooking time 5 minutes

12 large oysters

juice of ½ lemon

freshly ground black pepper

60ml double cream

1 slice white bread, made into
fine breadcrumbs

special equipment

an oyster knife

Preheat the grill to high and arrange a grill shelf about 10cm from the element.

Open the oysters according to the instructions on page 18, loosen them from their shells and arrange them, still in their shells, on the baking tray. Sprinkle over the lemon juice and grind some black pepper over each oyster. Then place 1 tsp double cream and a sprinkling of breadcrumbs into each oyster.

Place the oysters under the grill. Be watchful, as the shells occasionally crack and explode. Grill for 3 minutes, or until the crumbs are just brown and the oysters are bubbling. Serve immediately.

OYSTERS FRIED IN OATMEAL

✳ Serves 4 ✳ Preparation time 15 minutes ✳ Cooking time 2 minutes

This dish is a treat to make for good friends who are happy to graze in the kitchen, and it requires little formality.

12 top size oysters

50g medium oatmeal

50g clarified butter
(see glossary)

freshly ground black pepper

lemon wedges, to serve

Tabasco sauce, to serve

special equipment

an oyster knife

Shell the oysters following the instructions on page 18.

Remove the oysters in whole pieces from their shells and pat dry with kitchen paper. Season each one lightly with a grinding of black pepper. Spread the oatmeal on a plate and line another plate with kitchen paper. Roll the oysters in the oats to coat them completely.

Place a frying pan over a high heat, add the butter and, when it is foaming, add the oysters one at a time. By the time the last is in the pan the first should be ready to turn. Continue cooking and turning them until the oatmeal is a golden brown. Remove to the lined plate for a moment to drain, then serve on the shell with a squeeze of lemon or a few drops of Tabasco sauce.

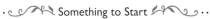
SHALLOT DRESSING FOR OYSTERS

✳ Makes enough for 24 oysters ✳ Preparation and chilling time 1 hour 5 minutes

**1 medium shallot, peeled
and very finely diced**

20ml red wine vinegar

30ml cider vinegar

Mix all the ingredients together in a bowl. Cover with cling film and and chill for a minimum of 1 hour or up to 24 hours before using. Serve with raw oysters.

'The French assert that the English oysters, which are esteemed the best in Europe, were originally procured from Cancalle Bay, near St Malo; but they assign no proof for this. It is a fact, however, that the oysters eaten in ancient Rome were nourished in the channel which then parted the Isle of Thanet from England, and which has since been filled up, and converted into meadows.'

Beeton's Book of Household Management

SMOKED,
SOUSED &
POTTED

SOUSED MACKEREL

✳ Serves 8-12 ✳ Preparation and cooking time 3-4 hours plus cooling overnight ✳ Pickling time 3 days

Many of the fish Mrs Beeton wrote about are simply not available to us today in quantity, but mackerel are still caught in large numbers in the summer from many small day boats around our coastline. If you come across a glut of fish, this recipe will preserve them for up to one month. You will need to make the brine on one day, and then allow it to cool before brining and pickling the fish the following day. Mrs Beeton's pickled mackerel recipe uses boiled fish, but today we are accustomed to the softer, fresher texture of uncooked fish in delicacies ranging from smoked salmon to sushi. If you are concerned about safety, the fish can be frozen for a week before pickling to kill off any parasites.

120g Maldon or other flaky sea salt

4 bay leaves

1 tbsp coriander seeds

½ tbsp allspice berries

1 tbsp juniper berries

1 tsp black peppercorns

1 tbsp sugar

zest of ½ lemon, sliced into strips

500ml cider vinegar

120g shallots, finely sliced

16 mackerel fillets

special equipment

a ceramic or glass baking dish large enough to hold all the fish and the pickling liquid

To make the brine, place 600ml water in a large pan over a high heat and add the salt. Bring to a simmer for 2 minutes, then cover and cool to room temperature.

To make the pickle, add 250ml cold water to a large pan over a high heat. Stir in all the remaining ingredients except the shallots and the mackerel and bring to a boil. Remove from the heat, leave to cool then add the shallots. Cover and reserve.

When the brine is cold, arrange the fish in the baking dish and pour over the brine. Leave for 2-3 hours to allow the fish to firm up, then remove the fish and pat it dry on kitchen paper. Discard the brine.

Rinse out the dish and arrange the fish in it in a double layer. Pour over the pickle and cover with cling film. Chill and keep in the fridge for at least 3 days before using. Use within 1 month of making. Serve with a salad of cucumber and Granny Smith apples or soured cream and malted bread.

SMOKED HADDOCK COCOTTES

❋ Serves 4 ❋ Preparation time 10 minutes ❋ Cooking time 13-20 minutes

The best smoked haddock is only lightly cured so that the sweet perfection of the flesh is not lost. Finnan haddock, which originates in the Aberdeenshire village of Findon, was named by Mrs Beeton as the finest expression of this particular fish, and it can still be found today. She cooked it in water with herbs, but to make a little go a long way it is paired here with cream and eggs and served in ramekins.

120g undyed smoked haddock, skinned and cut into small chunks

freshly ground black pepper

8 tbsp double cream

4 medium eggs

4 tsp grated Parmesan

special equipment

4 ramekins and a roasting tin

Preheat the oven to 160°C/gas mark 3. Divide the fish equally between the ramekins, grind over a little black pepper and add 1 tbsp of double cream to each ramekin.

Fill and boil the kettle. Place the ramekins in the roasting tin and pour boiling water around them to a depth of 2.5cm. Carefully transfer to the oven and cook them for 5 minutes. Remove the tin from the oven and crack a fresh egg into each ramekin. Add another tablespoon of double cream, a grinding of black pepper and a little Parmesan to each. Return to the oven for 13-15 minutes for a soft egg or 16-20 minutes for a set one. Serve immediately.

POTTED KIPPER

❋ Serves 4-6 ❋ Preparation time 35 minutes ❋ Cooking time 10 minutes

for the potting butter

200g unsalted butter

6 blades mace

¼ fresh nutmeg, grated

1 bay leaf

zest of ½ lemon, cut in strips

for the kipper

375g jugged kipper meat – about 2 kippers (see page 44)

½ tsp lemon juice

freshly ground black pepper

warm toast and lemon wedges, to serve

Place the butter, mace, grated nutmeg, bay leaf and lemon zest in a small pan over a medium heat and warm until the butter begins to bubble. Remove from the heat, cover and leave to infuse in a warm place for 30 minutes. Once infused, pour the butter through a sieve into a bowl, being careful to leave behind the milky liquid, known as solids, in the pan. Stir gently to distribute the butter evenly.

When the butter has nearly finished infusing, flake the kipper into a small serving bowl, carefully removing any small bones. Add the black pepper and lemon juice. Taste and add a little more of either ingredient if you would like.

Pour over the potting butter and mix it in, pressing the fish down into the butter. Cover and chill for up to 4 days. Serve this with toast and lemon wedges.

POTTED SALMON

* Serves 4 * Preparation time 35 minutes * Cooking time 10 minutes

1 quantity potting butter
(see potted kipper recipe, page 39)

375g poached salmon

1 tsp lemon juice

salt and freshly ground
black pepper

warm toast and lemon
wedges, to serve

Make the potting butter and leave it to infuse for 30 minutes. When it has nearly finished infusing, flake the salmon into a small serving dish with the lemon juice, ½ tsp salt and some black pepper and mix gently to combine.

Pour the potting butter over the salmon, pressing the fish to keep it under the surface of the butter. Cover and chill for up to 4 days. It is delicious served with warm toast and lemon wedges.

POTTED SHRIMPS

* Serves 4 * Preparation time 35 minutes * Cooking time 10 minutes

1 quantity potting butter
(see potted kipper recipe, page 39)

250g peeled cooked brown shrimps

2 tsp lemon juice

salt and freshly ground
black pepper

Make the potting butter and leave it to infuse for 30 minutes. When it has nearly finished infusing, place the shrimps snugly in a bowl and season with the lemon juice and black pepper. Check for saltiness. If the shrimps have not been salted add ½ tsp salt. Mix well to combine.

Pour the potting butter over the shrimps and stir to coat the shrimps, then press down. Cover and refrigerate until required. Eat within 4 days, served with bread.

Potted Fish and Shellfish

Potting meat and fish is a lovely way of making something special with leftovers, and the methods we use today are still identical to those used by Mrs Beeton. When potting meat it is often cooked immersed in fat, which acts to preserve the flesh for some time in the same manner as a confit of duck or pork. Fish, on the other hand, is more usually mixed with a seasoned butter, which is used to season the flesh rather than to preserve it. The result is an assertively flavoured delight that is perfect for a supper, lunch or picnic.

The meat pastes of my youth came in small jars from my grandparent's shop and were intense, if slightly inferior versions of what you can make at home.

Why is it, I wonder, that our meat pastes have suffered by comparison to their continental cousins, the pates? I am certain that the issue is their core ingredients. Well-sourced, beautifully cooked meat and fish leave scraps which, when amalgamated with butter (or lard) and seasonings, are excellent in flavour and super to use in sandwich fillings, or on toast. Poor quality ingredients, however, should be avoided.

I grew up by the shore in rural East Yorkshire where shrimping in shallow pools is still common. As the sea has warmed, we have begun to catch large species but it is the brown shrimp that we hunt for as it has the finest flavour. Grey-pink when cooked it is rightly prized across the UK and Europe. In the recipe opposite, we pot it with spice and citrus and it lends itself to no finer accompaniment than warm toast and perhaps a light ale.

STEAMED,
POACHED &
BOILED

JUGGED KIPPER

✳ Serves 1 ✳ Preparation time 5 minutes ✳ Cooking time 10 minutes

This method, an alternative to grilling, allows you to enjoy a kipper without filling your house with the smell of smoked fish.

1 kipper on the bone weighing 250g, head and tail removed

10g unsalted butter, softened

1 lemon wedge, to serve

special equipment

a large freezer bag and a 2-litre jug tall enough to hold the length of the kipper

Warm a plate in a low oven. Place the kipper head first into the freezer bag, then place the sealed bag into the jug, with the end sticking out beyond the rim of the jug.

Fill and boil the kettle. Pour boiling water into the jug around the outside of the bag so that the kipper is immersed but does not actually get wet. Leave for 10 minutes, then transfer the kipper onto the warmed serving plate and spread the softened butter on top. Serve with the lemon wedge.

CRAB FRESHLY BOILED WITH MAYONNAISE

✳ Serves 2 ✳ Cooking, cooling and preparation time 3 hours

A freshly cooked crab is one of the delights of the British seaside. A light white wine and good bread is the only accompaniment you need for a memorable summer lunch. If you have a live crab that you would like to cook yourself, see the instructions on page 17.

½ quantity mayonnaise
(see page 78), to serve

1 fresh cooked crab
weighing 1kg

½ tsp Worcestershire sauce

½ tsp brandy

6 drops Tabasco sauce

lemon juice, plus lemon
wedges, to serve

salt and freshly ground
black pepper

special equipment

a small hammer

Make the mayo a little ahead of time and chill until ready to serve. Place the crab upside down, facing away from you. Pull the claws gently towards you to remove. Crack them carefully with a small hammer and put the white meat in a small bowl.

Using a blunt knife, prise the body part of the shell away from the top part. The body contains white meat and a little dark, and has a number of pointed grey gills running up its sides, known as dead men's fingers. Remove these and discard them. Using a metal skewer, ease the meat from the tunnels in the body and spoon the dark meat and the light meat into separate bowls, being sure to discard any bits of shell. Spoon the brown meat from the upper shell.

A 1kg crab should yield 240g claw meat, 80g white meat and 130g brown meat. Hen crabs will yield more body meat; cocks more claw meat. The amount of brown meat depends on what moulting stage the crab was at. If a soft new shell is forming within the body cavity, there will be more. Soft new shell is edible – simply mash it with the remainder of the brown meat.

To present the crab, clean the upper shell then make the cavity larger by pressing against the rim of the hole until a segment of shell breaks cleanly away (see illustration). Do this on both sides of the shell. Pile the white meat back into the shell, leaving a space in the middle. Season the brown meat with the Worcestershire sauce, brandy and Tabasco sauce, adding black pepper and lemon juice to taste. Mash to a rough paste and pile into the space in the centre. Serve with the lemon wedges and mayonnaise.

MUSSELS IN WHITE WINE & GARLIC

❋ Serves 2 ❋ Preparation time 15 minutes ❋ Cooking time 5 minutes

Shellfish such as mussels are much more highly prized today than they were in 1861 when Isabella first collected the recipes for her book. Many people love them today – and given the cleaner waters we now find around our coastlines, they are easily grown or collected from rocky shorelines. Steamed quickly with aromatics, they are affordable as a weekday snack while offering you the flavour value of a weekend treat

1.2kg fresh mussels, beards removed and rinsed

150ml dry light white wine

2 shallots, peeled and finely chopped

2 garlic cloves, peeled and chopped

20g unsalted butter cut into 4 chunks

1 big bunch parsley, washed and finely chopped

black pepper to taste

Heat a wide, heavy-bottomed pan on a high flame to get it hot.

Place the mussels in a bowl with the wine, shallots, garlic and butter and when the pan is hot, tip the contents of the bowl into the hot pan to release a huge gush of steam. Put the lid on immediately – take care at this point not to have your face too near to the pan – and give the pan a shake to move the contents around.

Shake every 30 seconds for 3 minutes then remove the lid. At this point the mussels should be perfectly cooked and will have opened.

Add the parsley and black pepper, stir to combine and tip into a large serving dish.

Note: You can substitute a lovely dry cider for the white wine. In this case, add a splash of double cream to the pot when the mussels are cooked and stir to amalgamate.

POACHED BRILL
WITH BROWN SHRIMP BEURRE BLANC

✳ Serves 4 as a starter or 2 as a main course ✳ Preparation time 5 minutes ✳ Cooking time 30 minutes

This recipe strikes a marvellous balance of delicacy and richness. Fishmongers sell brown shrimps ready-peeled in small packets. At a pinch, you can buy potted shrimps and melt them out of their lovely butter and use them instead. Alternatively, as Mrs Beeton suggests, if you are lucky enough to have a lobster to hand, some of the coral head meat can be blended into the sauce to flavour it.

1 quantity court bouillon
(see page 75)

1 quantity beurre blanc
(see page 71) or fish cream sauce
(see page 70)

1 whole brill weighing 1kg,
skin and head removed

10g unsalted butter

100g peeled brown shrimps

lemon halves, to serve

special equipment

a temperature probe

Prepare the court bouillon and set it aside. Make the beurre blanc or fish cream sauce and keep it warm. If you are using beurre blanc place it in a bowl suspended over a pan of warm water. Cover it with a thick tea towel, and stir occasionally to ensure that it does not split.

Turn the oven on to low and set five plates inside to warm. Place the brill into a large, deep frying pan just big enough to hold it. Pour over the bouillon and bring to a simmer over a medium heat. Leave to cook gently for 12–15 minutes, then turn the heat off under the pan but leave the pan on the hob for a further 6–7 minutes. If you have a temperature probe, the fish should register 60°C at its thickest part. If it is colder than 55°C, leave it in the hot bouillon for another 5 minutes.

When the fish is cooked lift it from the pan, allow it to drain and transfer it to a warmed dish to rest for 5 minutes. Meanwhile, melt the butter in a small saucepan over a medium heat. Add the shrimps and cook until they begin to sizzle. Drain in a sieve and add to the beurre blanc or fish cream sauce, stirring to combine. Carefully remove the cooked fish to a board and, using a palette knife, remove each of the top 2 fillets that run lengthways along the backbone. Set each fillet onto a warmed plate. Repeat with the bottom 2 fillets and set them onto the other 2 plates. Pour over the sauce and serve with the lemon halves, and steamed greens.

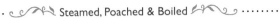
RAY WITH BROWN BUTTER, CAPERS & PARSLEY

❋ Serves 4 ❋ Preparation time 10 minutes ❋ Cooking time 20 minutes

Mrs Beeton gives a recipe for skate with capers, but since skate is rare today, this recipe has been modified for use with ray. This classic method of poaching ray is beautiful and here a court bouillon is used to flavour the flesh delicately, rather than the basic water and herb mixture that Mrs Beeton used. Look for thick portions of ray wings because they cook more evenly in their poaching liquor. The capers add a tangy flavour to the browned butter, with lemon adding a fresh citrus note as the fish is served.

1 quantity court bouillon
(see page 75)

4 x 200g portions ray wings

bunch parsley, stalks removed and reserved, leaves finely chopped

100g unsalted butter

4 tbsp baby capers,
finely chopped

100g unsalted butter

1 lemon, quartered

salt and freshly ground
black pepper

special equipment

a large, ovenproof serving dish and
a temperature probe

Make the court bouillon and chill until needed. Remove the fish from the fridge and leave, covered, at room temperature for half an hour before cooking.

Place a large serving dish in a low oven. Place the parsley stalks in the bottom of a large frying pan and arrange the fillets on top. Pour over the cold court bouillon, cover with a lid and place on a medium to high heat. Bring up to almost simmering, which should take about 8 minutes, then turn the fish and remove from the heat. Leave, covered with a lid, for a minimum of 5 minutes, to allow the fish continue to cook. A probe inserted in the fish should read about 60°C. If it is less than 50°C, leave the fish in the warm water for a further 5 minutes.

Once cooked, remove the fish from the liquid and drain. Place on the warm serving dish, sprinkle with a little salt and black pepper and keep warm in the oven while you make the butter sauce.

Place the butter in a small pan over a high heat until it sizzles, foams, turns brown and smells nutty. Just before it burns, toss in the capers and parsley and remove from the heat. Pour the foaming butter over the fish and serve immediately with the lemon wedges.

SHELLFISH BISQUE

✻ Serves 4–6 ✻ Preparation time 5 minutes ✻ Cooking time 15 minutes

This thick, creamy soup is a classic and is great with crusty bread as a luxurious lunch or a sumptuous start to dinner.

50g unsalted butter

50g onion, peeled and chopped

50g leek, chopped

50g carrot, peeled and chopped

50g celery, chopped

1 litre shellfish stock (see page 72)

125ml double cream

300g cooked crab or lobster meat (optional)

salt, to taste

Place the butter in a saucepan over a medium heat. Add the onion, leek, carrot and celery and cook gently for 10–15 minutes, until the vegetables are soft.

Add the shellfish stock and bring to a simmer for 10 minutes. Don't let it boil as this will ruin the delicate flavour. Strain to remove the vegetables.

Put the liquid back into the clean pan and set on a medium heat. Warm the soup to a very gentle simmer, add in the double cream, then taste for seasoning, adding a little salt if necessary. Simmer until you are satisfied with the flavour but there is still enough for 4–6 shallow soup bowls.

Stir through the fresh crab or lobster meat (if using), heat for another 2 minutes without boiling and serve immediately in warmed bowls. This is lovely garnished with sprigs of parsley or watercress.

POACHED LOBSTER

✳ Serves 2 as a starter ✳ Preparation time 5 minutes ✳ Cooking time 15 minutes per kg

If you come across really lively fresh lobsters, buy one and cook it for yourself – you will appreciate why people prize them so highly. There is some debate over whether crustaceans feel pain – with some arguing that the lobster has too simple a central nervous system to register stimuli. However, if you prefer not to drop a lively lobster straight into fast-boiling water, you can put it 'to sleep' in the freezer for 15 minute or so, prior to cooking. Or pierce a knife in its head, just before cooking, to kill it instantly (see page 18). Whatever method you choose, be sure to get the timings right. As Mrs Beeton advised, fresh-cooked lobster should have 'a stiffness in the tail, which, if gently raised, will return with a spring'.

1 live lobster weighing 650–750g

1½tsp salt

Calculate your cooking time at 15 minutes per kg – a 750g lobster, for example, needs 12 minutes. If you plan to cook more than 1 lobster you can either use 2 pans or you can cook up to 2 in a pan. Cooking more than 2 together will affect the cooking times.

Place 4 litres of water in a large pan over a high heat. Add the salt and bring to a rapid boil with the lid on. Transfer the lobster to the boiling water. Cover the pan but don't let it boil over. Once it returns to a rapid boil, adjust the heat to a simmer. Time the cooking of the lobster from the moment the water begins to simmer. While it is cooking fill a large bowl with ice and water.

When the lobster is cooked remove it from the pot using long-handled tongs and plunge it into the bowl of iced water for 10 minutes. Drain the bowl, rinse the lobster briefly under cold water then chill until required.

To prepare the lobster for the table, cut it in half lengthways with a large, sharp knife. Open up the halves. You will notice that the head cavity contains some brown meat. This is delicious. It also contains a clear stomach sac that may have some contents depending on when the animal last ate. Remove any parts of this from both halves. Next look at the

lobster's tail meat. Just under the outer rim of the shell you should see a long narrow intestinal tube extending the full length of the tail. Remove this carefully and discard it. Wipe the white tail meat with a damp piece of kitchen paper to remove any particles of debris. The lobster is now ready to eat. You can serve it with homemade mayonnaise (see page 78), clarified butter (see glossary) or lemon wedges, and a light fruity Muscadet or perhaps a dry Riesling or Chablis to drink.

'In its element, the lobster is able to run with great speed upon its legs, or small claws, and, if alarmed, to spring, tail foremost, to a considerable distance, even, it is said, "with the swiftness of a bird flying". Fishermen have seen some of them pass about thirty feet with a wonderful degree of swiftness. When frightened, they will take their spring, and, like a chamois of the Alps, plant themselves upon the very spot upon which they designed to hold themselves.'

Beeton's Book of Household Management

GRILLED
& BAKED

GRILLED KIPPER

* Serves 1 * Preparation time 2 minutes * Cooking time 5–7 minutes

The migratory herring carried with it the fortunes of many eastern coastal towns, with large numbers of men and women catching and processing the huge shoals in difficult conditions until gradually fish numbers declined and the value of the harvest no longer made it worthwhile. These 'silver darlings' were more often salted or smoked than eaten fresh simply because of the sheer numbers caught. Split and smoked, they are called kippers, while those with their guts intact and lightly smoked are known as bloaters, famously produced in Great Yarmouth. Mrs Beeton included a recipe for Yarmouth bloaters, but today it is the kipper that is most popular and widely available, hence the substitution.

1 kipper on the bone weighing 250g, head and tail removed

10g unsalted butter, softened

1 lemon wedge, to serve

Preheat the grill to medium. Position the top shelf about 10–15cm from the grill element and place a serving plate under the top shelf to warm. Line a baking tray with foil.

Place the kipper skin-side down onto the lined tray. Spread the butter over the fish and place under the grill for 5–7 minutes. Serve on the warmed plate with the lemon wedge.

DOVER SOLE
GRILLED WITH WHITE WINE & LEMON

✳ Serves 2 ✳ Preparation time 5 minutes ✳ Cooking time 8–10 minutes

Here is a very smart yet simple way to serve this meaty and delicious flatfish. Mrs Beeton often advised her readers to blanch fish first in boiling water to remove impurities. This can result in overcooked fish if you are not careful, so it is best to cook the fish as suggested here.

40g softened unsalted butter, plus extra for greasing

1 Dover sole weighing 600g, skinned, head removed if preferred

juice of ½ lemon

70ml light fruity white wine such as Muscadet

salt and freshly ground black pepper

special equipment

a large, ovenproof serving dish

Preheat the grill to hot, and set the top shelf 10–15cm from the grill element. Place a large serving dish below the rack to warm. Line a baking tray with foil and grease with a little butter.

Season the fish lightly on both sides with salt and black pepper and place on the baking tray with the thickest side uppermost. Dot the butter onto the fish and pour over the lemon juice and white wine. Grill for 4–5 minutes on one side, then turn carefully with a fish slice and grill on the other side until lightly browned and cooked through. The fish is cooked when the meat pulls away from the bones eaily with a fork.

Transfer to the serving dish, pour over the cooking juices and serve immediately.

GRILLED MACKEREL
WITH GOOSEBERRY SAUCE

✳ Serves 4 ✳ Preparation time 15 minutes ✳ Cooking time 25 minutes

Inspired by Mrs Beeton's gooseberry sauce for boiled mackerel, this is an unusual combination, but a good one: the sharpness of the gooseberries cuts through the richness of the fish. In the early summer, both mackerel and gooseberries appear in our markets, though you could easily go and catch a mackerel yourself just by trailing a line off a pier. Mackerel must be cooked as soon as possible because it deteriorates more quickly than any other fish.

300g green gooseberries, topped and tailed

½ tbsp white wine vinegar

3 tbsp sugar

½ shallot, finely chopped

4 whole mackerel, gutted

4 tbsp light olive oil

salt and freshly ground black pepper

Put four plates into a low oven to warm. Line a baking tray large enough to hold all the fish in one layer with foil and set aside.

Put all of the ingredients except for the fish, olive oil and seasoning into a small saucepan over a low heat along with 4 tbsp water. Simmer gently, stirring occasionally, for 15–20 minutes, or until the berries are broken down and tender. Crush any whole berries with a fork and remove the sauce from the heat. Cover and keep warm until needed.

Meanwhile, preheat the grill to high and arrange the shelf about 15cm from the element. Dry the mackerel well with kitchen paper and make 3–4 diagonal slits in each side of the fish. Rub the skins lightly with the oil and season all over with salt and black pepper. Arrange the fish on the prepared tray and grill for 5 minutes, then turn the fish over and grill for a further 3–5 minutes.

The fish is ready when the flesh is firm to the touch and can be eased away from the bone with a fork, or when a temperature probe inserted into the fattest part reads 60°C or more. Serve the fish with the sauce on the side.

GRILLED LOBSTER
WITH PARSLEY & GARLIC BUTTER

✳ Serves 4 ✳ Preparation time 15 minutes ✳ Cooking time 15 minutes

Lobster was relatively expensive even in Mrs Beeton's day but nonetheless she gave many recipes for it, often chopping or pounding the flesh then cooking it with cream or flavoured mixtures. Here, her version of maître d'hôtel butter is used to baste the flesh as it cooks.

100g parsley & garlic butter
(see page 82)

2 tbsp melted unsalted butter,
for greasing

½ tsp salt

2 lobsters weighing 650–750g each,
freshly killed (see page 18 or ask
your fishmonger to do this for you)

4 slices crusty bread

lemon wedges, to serve

special equipment

a small hammer

Make the parsley and garlic butter and chill until needed. Line the baking tray with foil, grease and set aside.

Place a pan over a high heat and add 1 litre of water. Bring to a boil, turn down to a simmer then add the salt, stirring to dissolve. Remove the claws from the lobsters by pulling them backwards gently until they come away from the body. Add these to the pan and simmer for 5 minutes. Meanwhile, fill a large bowl with ice and water. Remove the claws from the pot using long-handled tongs and plunge them into the icy water for 5 minutes. Once the claws are cool, rinse them under cold water, then crack them open using a large spoon or small hammer. Remove the meat, preferably in whole pieces, and set aside.

Preheat the grill to high and place the shelf 10–15cm from the element. Cut the lobsters in half lengthways and remove the stomach sacs from the head cavities. Leave any pale brown and dark green matter in place – this is edible and will turn red when cooked. Place the lobster halves cut-side down on the prepared baking tray and grill for 5 minutes.

Turn the halves over. Fill the head cavities with the claw meat and spread the parsley and garlic butter all over. Grill for a further 3–4 minutes, until browned and sizzling.

Place a piece of crusty bread on each plate and top with half a lobster. Drizzle over the cooking juices and serve immediately with lemon wedges and a simple green salad.

LEMON SOLE GRILLED WITH CREAM & MACE

✳ Serves 4 as a starter or 2 as a light main course ✳ Preparation time 10 minutes
✳ Cooking time 15 minutes

This is a very simple, absolutely delicious, way of cooking sole but it also works with other small flatfish like dabs and plaice. Mrs Beeton clearly liked to use mace as a fish seasoning: its sharp piquancy adds a spicy note to the delicate flavour of the fish and cream.

30g butter

300ml double cream

1 large pinch ground mace

zest of ¼ lemon

½ tsp salt

2 x 400g whole lemon sole, skinned and heads removed

special equipment

a large, oval flameproof dish

Melt the butter in the dish, rolling it around to thoroughly coat the inside surface, then set aside. Preheat the grill to high and position the shelf 10–15cm from the element.

Warm the cream in a small pan over a medium heat. Stir in the mace, lemon zest and salt.

Place both fish, thickest side uppermost, on the prepared dish and pour the cream sauce over them. Grill for 5–7 minutes on one side, spooning the sauce over occasionally. Turn the fish carefully and grill on the other side for a further 3–4 minutes. The sauce will reduce to a thick savoury cream. The fish is cooked when the flesh pulls away from the bone cleanly with a fork. At this point, turn the grill off and let the fish rest for 3–4 minutes before serving.

WHOLE BAKED SALMON

✳ Serves 10–15 ✳ Preparation time 10 minutes
✳ Cooking time 1 hour 30 minutes–2 hours plus 30 minutes resting time

A whole salmon makes an impressive party centrepiece. Mrs Beeton boils hers in a fish kettle, but this method for baking the fish on an oven tray achieves a similar result. You will need a wide roll of foil to parcel it up.

1 whole salmon weighing 4kg, head and tail removed

sunflower oil, for brushing

1 tbsp Maldon or other flaky sea salt or 2 tsp fine salt

1 small, unwaxed lemon, thickly sliced

special equipment

wide foil, a very large, deep baking tray and a temperature probe

Preheat the oven to 140°C/gas mark 1. Place the salmon on a large sheet of foil and brush the skin with the oil. Sprinkle a few pinches of salt inside the body cavity, insert the lemon slices, then place the salmon on its belly on the foil and sprinkle all over with salt. Seal the foil around the salmon, pinching the edges together to ensure there are no gaps, then place in a large roasting tin, curving the fish to fit if necessary.

Pour enough boiling water into the tin to come 2.5cm up the side and place in the oven for 1½–2 hours. After this time a temperature probe inserted into the thickest part of the fish should register 45–50°C. If not, cook for a further 15–20 minutes and retest. Remove from the oven and leave parcelled up in a warm place to rest for 30 minutes.

If you are planning to eat the salmon hot, open the parcel and skin the fish. Using a small knife, scrape the brown meat from the sides and discard. Slip the salmon onto a serving dish and serve with a double quantity of hollandaise sauce (see page 76) or fish cream sauce (see page 70).

If you are planning to eat the salmon cold, chill it briefly after resting. Then remove the skin and scrape the brown meat from the sides of the fish. Discard all the debris and transfer to a serving dish. If you are preparing this a day ahead, cover with cling film and chill overnight, but allow it to come up to a cool room temperature for an hour before eating. Dress the fish with watercress salad (see page 86) and some homemade mayonnaise (see page 78) or soured cream.

FISH PIE

✳ Serves 4-6   ✳ Preparation time 1 hour   ✳ Cooking time 25–30 minutes

Mrs Beeton used cod and oysters in her fish pie, a delicious mixture but one that is now rather expensive for a kitchen-supper dish. The smoked haddock used here instead adds piquancy to the delicate pollock or coley, with a few prawns added for succulence.

for the mashed potatoes

650–700g peeled Maris piper or King Edward potatoes, cut into 3cm cubes

10g salt

130g butter

1 tbsp milk

salt and freshly ground black pepper

for the fish pie

500ml milk

1 bay leaf

1 small carrot, cut in half

½ onion, cut into large chunks

1 tsp black peppercorns

400g pollock or coley fillet

100g smoked undyed haddock

approx. 150ml double cream

50g unsalted butter

50g plain flour

freshly grated nutmeg, to taste

50g prawns

1 tbsp melted unsalted butter

salt, to taste

to garnish

small bunch fresh parsley, tough stems discarded, leaves chopped

1 tarragon sprig, stem discarded, leaves finely chopped

special equipment

1.5-litre ovenproof dish and a temperature probe

Place the potatoes in a large saucepan, add enough water to cover and the salt. Bring to a boil over a high heat, then reduce the heat and simmer very gently for about 20 minutes, checking them regularly with a sharp knife. As soon as they are tender, remove from the heat.

Drain through a large colander. To ensure any excess water is driven off, leave the potatoes to sit, uncovered, until quite dry and still warm, then return them to the pan.

Melt the butter in a small pan over a medium heat. When it is hot and foaming add the milk and stir, then pour the mixture over the potatoes. Turn the heat under the potatoes to medium and mash them with a potato masher to break them up, then beat them with a wooden spoon until light and fluffy. Alternatively, melt the butter in a larger pan and then press the potatoes through a ricer onto the hot butter and milk, beating after that with a wooden spoon. Adjust the seasoning to taste, and set aside.

Place the milk, bay leaf, carrot, onion and peppercorns in a saucepan and bring to a boil. Turn off the heat and allow to infuse for 15 minutes. Strain the milk into another pan that is large enough to hold

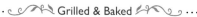

the fish, and discard the other ingredients. Bring the liquid to a simmer over a medium heat. Add the fish and simmer for 2 minutes, then turn the heat off and leave to sit for 10 minutes. Set the fish aside, strain the milk into a measuring jug and make up to 500ml with the double cream. Pour the milk and cream mixture into a saucepan over a low heat and bring to a simmer.

Meanwhile, make a roux by melting 50g butter in a small pan over a medium heat. Add the flour and cook, stirring, for 3–5 minutes, or until the mixture begins to foam, taking care that it does not burn. Turn the heat to low and whisk the milk mixture into the roux a little at a time, then simmer for 3–4 minutes, or until the sauce is glossy, silky and free of lumps. If it tastes floury, cook it for another 1–2 minutes. Season to taste with nutmeg and a little salt.

Preheat the oven to 180°C/gas mark 4 and line a baking tray with foil. Flake the cooked fish into the ovenproof dish, scatter over the prawns and pour over the sauce. Spoon the mashed potatoes on top, starting at the edge of the dish and working inwards.

Brush the pie with the butter, place it on the baking tray and bake in the centre of the oven for 25–30 minutes. The pie is cooked when it is bubbling around the edges, or when a temperature probe inserted in the centre reads 85°C. If the surface of the pie is still pale in colour at this stage, place it under a hot grill to brown the top. Serve immediately, sprinkling the herbs over each portion as you hand it round.

STOCKS
& SAUCES

FISH CREAM SAUCE

Serves 4 · Preparation time 15 minutes · Cooking time 45 minutes

Mrs Beeton's cream sauce for fish is a simple mixture of cream with salt, cayenne, and a little mace or lemon juice, thickened with butter and flour. She also suggests adding shallots for flavour. This updated version shows how this kind of sauce has developed over the intervening period, using fish stock, wine and vermouth to add layers of flavour. The result is a more rounded sauce that will appeal to the modern palate. Fennel and garlic, which were available but not well used in Victorian Britain, have also been added to the shallots as they pair well with fish.

- 150g fish bones, preferably flatfish
- 150g white fish trimmings
- 1 small carrot, peeled
- 1 small stick celery, trimmed
- 1 small piece fennel, trimmed
- ½ small onion, peeled and halved
- 2 tsp sunflower oil
- 100g shallot, peeled and finely sliced
- ½ bulb fennel, finely sliced
- 1 small garlic clove, peeled and finely sliced
- 1 bay leaf
- 50ml white wine
- 50ml dry white Vermouth (Noilly Prat), plus extra to serve
- 300ml double cream
- lemon juice, to taste
- 2 tbsp finely chopped fresh chervil, parsley or tarragon, to serve
- salt

First make the stock by placing the fish bones and trimmings and the pieces of carrot, celery, fennel and onion, along with 750ml cold water, into a pan over a medium heat. Bring the stock almost to simmering then turn the heat to low and cook for 20 minutes. Remove from the heat and pour through a fine sieve into a bowl, discard the bones and vegetables.

Pour the sunflower oil into a medium saucepan over a medium heat. Add the finely sliced shallot, fennel and garlic along with the bay leaf and cook gently until the vegetables are soft, but not coloured.

Add the white wine and Vermouth and cook until the liquid has almost all evaporated, then add the stock and simmer until reduced by three-quarters. Finally, add the double cream and cook until the liquid has reduced by half.

Season with lemon juice and salt to taste, then pass the mixture through a fine sieve into a sauceboat or serving jug. Just before serving, add ½ tbsp dry Vermouth and sprinkle over the finely chopped herbs.

BEURRE BLANC

✳ Serves 4 ✳ Preparation time 5 minutes ✳ Cooking time 15 minutes

This sauce, a French classic, is similar to Mrs Beeton's many butter sauces, but avoids the use of flour, so it is a really versatile and easy sauce to make. Use the best unsalted butter and you will find that it amalgamates more easily with the vinegary shallots.

1 large or 2 small shallots, peeled and finely sliced

100ml dry white wine

1 tbsp white wine vinegar

1 tbsp single cream

200g chilled unsalted butter, cut into 20 cubes

lemon juice, to taste

white pepper, to taste

Place the sliced shallot, wine and vinegar in a small stainless steel pan over a medium heat. Bring to a simmer and cook, stirring occasionally, until all of the liquid has evaporated. Whisk in the cream and turn the heat down very low, resting the pan on just half the ring to avoid overheating the sauce. Add the butter in chunks, beating rapidly to amalgamate until it is all incorporated and the sauce is smooth. Do not allow the butter to melt or turn to oil. If it does, throw in a small splash of cold water or an ice cube and beat well to emulsify. Strain the sauce through a fine sieve into a small pan, add a squeeze of lemon juice and a pinch of white pepper to taste, and serve immediately with poached or grilled fish. This sauce does not keep for more than 30 minutes.

SHELLFISH STOCK

❋ Makes 2 litres ❋ Preparation time 1 hour 30 minutes ❋ Cooking time 2–3 hours

This richly aromatic stock forms the foundation of delicious shellfish soups, such as the bisque on page 52. The best shells to use are those left from picking crab and lobster. A fishmonger who sells dressed crabs will usually be happy to save you some shells in the freezer. Roasting the shells intensifies the flavour.

2kg crab, lobster or prawn shells

2 tbsp sunflower oil

1 stick celery, roughly chopped

1 large onion, peeled and roughly chopped

1 medium carrot, peeled and roughly chopped

1 large tomato, roughly chopped

50ml brandy

300ml dry white Vermouth

500ml dry white wine

1 garlic clove, peeled and halved

2 bay leaves

1 large thyme sprig

Preheat the oven to 200°C/gas mark 6. Place the shells in the tin, drizzle over the oil and toss to coat, then set in the oven to roast. Stir occasionally until beginning to brown.

After 1 hour, add the celery, onion, carrot and tomato, and mix well. Roast for a further 30 minutes, stirring occasionally. Remove the tin from the oven and set on the cooker top.

Add the brandy to the tin and carefully set the mixture alight at the side of the tin using a match, tipping the liquid around the tin to catch all of the alcohol. Allow the flames to die down then add the wine and Vermouth. Stir the mixture together and scrape into the stockpot.

Pour in enough cold water to cover the shells to a depth of 10cm, then add the garlic and herbs to the pan and set over a high heat. Bring to a simmer, turn the heat down to low and cook for 3 hours. Strain the mixture into a bowl, then pour it back into the cleaned stockpot and simmer until it is reduced to about 2 litres.

FISH STOCK

* Makes 600ml * Preparation time 10 minutes * Cooking time 1 hour

Fish stocks require only light cooking. Cook them too much and you will produce glue. A variety of fish bones can be used, but flatfish bones are the most gelatinous. Sole or halibut bones provide the best flavour and produce the clearest stock.

30g unsalted butter

4 shallots, peeled and finely chopped

250ml light dry white wine such as Muscadet

500g fish bones (preferably sole or halibut), chopped into 4cm pieces

1 carrot, peeled and finely chopped

½ leek, split in half lengthways

1 bay leaf

a few parsley stalks

Place a large saucepan over a medium heat. Add the butter and then the shallots. Cook, stirring, for 4–5 minutes or until they are softened but not coloured.

Add the white wine and cook until it has reduced by half, then add the remaining ingredients. Pour in 700ml cold water and bring the mixture to a gentle simmer. Skim off any scum that rises to the surface.

Cook the stock on a low heat for 45 minutes, then remove from the heat and strain through a sieve into a large bowl. Discard the bones, vegetables and flavourings. Cover and chill the stock. Either use within 3–4 days or freeze in 250ml portions for up to 2 months.

Note: The boiled meat that you remove from your stock will be very tender and falling from the bone – but it can still be used. Shred it from the bones and chill, then mix with a seasoned mayonnaise for a sandwich filling.

COURT BOUILLON

✳ Makes 1.25 litres ✳ Preparation time 5 minutes ✳ Cooking time 30 minutes

This stock is used for poaching fish and delicate meats. It keeps the flesh moist while adding a lightly piquant flavour and is appropriate when a clean, subtle result is desired. It is only cooked for a short period of time to keep the flavours fresh.

1 carrot, peeled and chopped into chunks

1 stick celery, trimmed and chopped into chunks

1 medium onion, peeled and finely sliced

1 small leek, finely sliced

½ fennel bulb, finely sliced

½ lemon, finely sliced

2 thyme sprigs

2 garlic cloves, peeled and coarsely chopped

2 tsp black peppercorns

2–3 tarragon sprigs

small bunch parsley

200ml dry white wine

special equipment

a large stockpot

Place all the ingredients into the stockpot over a high heat. Add 1.3 litres of cold water, bring to a boil and simmer for 20 minutes. Pass immediately through muslin or a fine sieve into a bowl.

Discard the vegetables, cover the bouillon and chill or freeze in 250ml portions for up to 2 months.

HOLLANDAISE SAUCE

※ Serves 4 ※ Preparation time 15 minutes ※ Cooking time 10 to 15 minutes

Mrs Beeton's Dutch sauce for fish contains a lot less butter than this modern recipe, and a lot more acid (in the original both vinegar and lemon juice are used). Today, we prefer a less sharp sauce, and we commonly serve it not only with fish but also with vegetables such as asparagus, or poured over eggs.

250g unsalted butter

2 large egg yolks

½ tsp lemon juice

salt to taste

special equipment

**a heatproof glass
or ceramic bowl**

Place the butter in a small pan over a medium heat. When it has melted, turn the heat off and keep the pan warm to one side.

Place a heatproof glass or ceramic bowl over a pan of barely simmering water over a low to medium heat. Make sure that the base of the bowl does not touch the water.

Add the egg yolks and lemon juice to the bowl along with ½ tsp water, whisking continuously until they become pale and fluffy. Whisk the hot butter into the egg mixture a little at a time until it is fully incorporated. Continue to whisk until the sauce is thickened and hot. Remove the pan and bowl from the heat to stop it cooking any further and season to taste with a little salt. The sauce can be kept warm over the water for 30 minutes but then must be used, as it will not keep.

MAYONNAISE

* Serves 4 * Preparation time 10 minutes

Mrs Beeton noted that patience is needed to make this sauce well, and she is right. The liaison works only if each addition of oil is fully incorporated before more is added. You can experiment with the mix of oils – but using a majority of mild oil will keep the sauce light so that it does not overpower the rest of the meal.

1 very fresh whole egg
plus 1 yolk

a pinch of white pepper

½ tbsp Dijon mustard

1 tbsp white wine vinegar

1 scant tsp Maldon or other
sea salt, or ½ tsp fine salt

2 garlic cloves, peeled and crushed
(optional)

250ml light olive oil

3 tbsp water

50ml strong extra virgin
olive oil

lemon juice to taste

Place the whole egg and the extra yolk, pepper, mustard, vinegar, salt and the crushed garlic, if you are making garlic mayonnaise, into the bowl of a hand blender or a small liquidiser and whiz for 10 seconds until creamy. With the motor still running, slowly add the light olive oil in a thin stream, pausing every few seconds to allow the sauce to emulsify before you add more oil.

Continue until the oil is fully incorporated. You should notice that the sauce thickens as you go, and the mixture turns paler. Leave the machine running, add 3 tbsp water and mix for 2 minutes, then slowly add the extra virgin olive oil as before.

Add ½ tsp lemon juice and adjust to taste with a little more lemon juice and salt, if you like. To gain a finer texture, pass the mayonnaise through a sieve before serving.

For a firmer mayonnaise, add 50–100ml more extra virgin olive oil, then add a very little cold water to thin it to the consistency you desire. Store in the fridge in a sealed jar or covered closely with cling film, and eat within 2 days.

Note: Mayonnaise can split if too much oil is added at once. If this happens, the mixture will turn quickly from a thickening sauce to a liquid, oily mass. To rectify this, start with a clean bowl and add another egg yolk mixed with 1 tbsp tepid water. Beat the two together lightly and then, carefully, add the split mayo a little at a time, beating well with each addition.

ON THE
TABLE

PARSLEY & GARLIC BUTTER

❋ Makes 100g ❋ Preparation time 5 minutes

Mrs Beeton's parsley butter was suggested as an accompaniment to boiled fowls – which we rarely cook today. However, the addition of a little garlic turns the original recipe into a versatile butter for the modern kitchen. It is whipped to ensure that it does not run when heated.

100g softened unsalted butter

large bunch of parsley, leaves only, finely chopped

2 garlic cloves, finely chopped

½ tsp Maldon or other flaky salt

Place the butter in a medium-sized bowl and whip until creamy, pale and fluffy. Add the parsley, garlic and salt and whip until combined.

Cover and chill until required. It will keep for 2 days in the fridge.

ANCHOVY BUTTER

❋ Makes 100g ❋ Preparation time 5 minutes

This savoury butter is a good standby to have in the fridge and makes an excellent snack served spread over hot, white toast or over steamed vegetables with a squeeze of lemon juice on top.

60g anchovy fillets in oil

40g unsalted butter, softened

1 pinch each ground ginger, mace, cinnamon and freshly ground black pepper

10 drops Tabasco or other chilli sauce

Drain the anchovy fillets, then place all the ingredients in a mortar and pestle or into the jug of a small blender and blend to a smooth paste. Place in a dish or ramekin, cover with cling film and chill until required.

CUCUMBER & APPLE SALAD

✳ Serves 4 ✳ Preparation time 10 minutes

This salad, or relish, is excellent with fish, but it has modern origins. Isabella, in common with many of her contemporary writers, was as inclined to cook cucumber as she was to use it in salads. Steamed, it is lovely buttered and served with dill. However, in this fresh, modern approach, it serves as a sweet cool salad that makes an excellent accompaniment to smoked fish or seafood. Make it no more than half an hour before you intend to use it.

1 cucumber

1 tsp chopped dill

2 tbsp light olive oil

½ tbsp white wine or cider vinegar

a pinch of caster sugar

2 sharp-sweet English apples such as Cox's orange pippin

salt and freshly ground black pepper

Cut your cucumber into 15cm sections and peel each one as thinly as you can with a vegetable peeler or sharp knife. Then cut each section in half and, using a small spoon, scoop out the seeds. Discard these along with the peel.

Cut the peeled cucumber into 3mm slices and place in a medium bowl, then add the dill, olive oil, vinegar and a pinch of sugar, salt and black pepper.

Quarter the apple, then core and peel it. Cut the apple quarters into thin sections and toss with the cucumber mixture. Chill briefly before serving.

TARTARE SAUCE

✳ Serves 4–6   ✳ Preparation time 15 minutes

This chunky tartare sauce makes the perfect accompaniment to any white fish and is particularly lovely with lemon sole (see page 64).

1 quantity mayonnaise
(see page 78)

100g cornichons, drained
and chopped

100g capers, drained and chopped

1 small banana shallot, finely diced

1 small bunch parsley, chopped

a few sprigs tarragon, chopped

juice of 1 lemon

salt and freshly ground black
pepper

In a small mixing bowl, stir the cornichons, capers, shallot and chopped herbs into the mayonnaise. Add the lemon juice and season to taste. Chill in the fridge until ready to use.

WATERCRESS SALAD

✳ Serves 4 ✳ Preparation time 10 minutes

Watercress and many other wild plants were so commonly collected and used historically that we rarely see recipes for them – they are simply taken for granted. Hampshire watercress came to prominence when the railways brought crops into the London markets at around the time Mrs Beeton's book was published, and it is still the best. This flavourful strong leaf is an ideal accompaniment to any game or meat dish.

4 large handfuls fresh watercress

3 tbsp extra virgin olive oil

juice of ¼ lemon

pinch sea salt

Place the watercress in a large bowl of iced water, and then pick the pieces out, discarding any tough stems as you go. Transfer the leaves to a salad spinner. Just before you are ready to serve, give the leaves a spin to dry them then place them in a salad bowl. Drizzle over the olive oil, a good squeeze of lemon and a little salt. Toss gently to coat and serve.

GRILLED MUSHROOM FLAPS

✳ Serves 4 ✳ Preparation time 5 minutes ✳ Cooking time 8–10 minutes

Mrs Beeton noted that large mushroom flaps (or tops) are best for this recipe, while she reserved button mushrooms for stews. Of course, you can use whichever you prefer, but the larger, mature mushrooms do have a more intense, almost animal flavour. You can grill them simply with butter and perhaps a sprinkle of lemon juice, as in the original recipe, but the addition of garlic gives a rich, savoury flavour.

8 large, flat field mushrooms, each about 8–10cm in diameter

2 tbsp olive oil, for brushing

½ quantity parsley & garlic butter (see page 82)

salt and freshly ground black pepper

Preheat the grill to high. Peel the mushrooms and remove their stalks. Place them on a baking tray in a single layer, gill-side down. Brush the caps with the olive oil, season with a light sprinkling of salt and place under the grill at a distance of no less than 10cm from the element. Cook until the mushrooms start to collapse and turn golden brown. Flip them over, divide the parsley and garlic butter between the mushrooms, then place them back under the grill and cook for 2 minutes, or until the butter is foaming and beginning to colour. Serve immediately.

BUTTERED SPINACH

✳ Serves 4 ✳ Preparation time 10 minutes ✳ Cooking time 10 minutes

Spinach – which for Isabella could very well have meant an amalgam of summer greens
– makes an excellent accompaniment to fish. The sharp, tannic qualities of spinach are
softened by the addition of sweet butter and a little spice. To save time in your final
preparation, you can wilt and drain the leaves several hours in advance. The final reheating
and puréeing can be accomplished with little effort while your chosen fish cooks.

400g large leaf spinach

50g unsalted butter

salt and freshly ground black
pepper to taste

to finish

50–100g unsalted butter

a pinch of ground mace

First, wash your spinach. Fill a large bowl or sink with
enough cold water to allow the spinach to float and agitate
the leaves for a couple of minutes. Allow any dust or sand to
sediment out, and lift the leaves into a large colander. Repeat
if necessary. Allow the leaves to drain well – turn them over so
that the water can drain from them for 5 minutes.

Cook the spinach in 2 or 3 batches. First, heat a large, heavy
pan on a high heat, then drop in a couple of handfuls of
leaves, followed by a small pinch of salt and a generous knob
of butter. Stir the leaves as they steam in their own juices.
After a minute or so, the leaves will be all wilted and dark
green at which point tip them into a colander and drain. Rinse
out the pan and repeat until you have used up all the leaves.

When all your spinach is in the colander, press the wilted
leaves with the back of a ladle to extract as much liquid as
possible. If you like, you can chill the leaves for up to 4 hours
at this point.

To finish the spinach, place a clean pan on a low to medium
heat. Melt some butter (the more you use, the richer and
sweeter your dish will be), then stir in the greens, adding a
grind of pepper and a pinch of mace. When the leaves are hot,
transfer to the bowl of a blender and purée until you have a
silky, dark green mixture. (You can sieve the purée if you like
something really fine.) Return to a clean pan and reheat over
a low flame until piping hot. Serve alongside the fish of your
choice – mine would be the fish pie or the grilled lemon sole.

POTATOES A LA MAITRE D'HOTEL

❋ Serves 4 ❋ Preparation time 10 minutes ❋ Cooking time 25 minutes

Charlotte potatoes or small new potatoes, both of which have less starch than other varieties, are just right for making this special recipe. The 'maître d'hôtel' combination of butter, lemon and parsley is one of Mrs Beeton's most commonly used flavourings.

400g small Charlotte or new potatoes

3 tbsp light olive oil

50g butter

1 banana shallot, peeled and chopped

100ml chicken stock

finely grated zest of ½ lemon

large handful flat-leaf parsley, stems discarded, leaves finely chopped

salt and freshly ground black pepper

Place the potatoes in a large pan over a high heat. Cover them with water and add a large pinch of salt. Bring to a boil and cook for 10 minutes, or until the potatoes are tender, then drain well. Place the oil in a large frying pan over a medium to heat and fry the potatoes for 5–7 minutes, or until they lightly browned on all sides. Stir them occasionally to prevent them burning.

Season the potatoes with salt and black pepper then reduce the heat and add the butter and shallot to the pan. Toss gently together for 2 minutes to cook the shallot then add the stock. Continue cooking until the liquid is reduced to a glaze.

Remove the pan from the heat and transfer the potatoes to a serving dish. Add the lemon zest and parsley and toss everything together gently to combine. Serve immediately.

PRODUCERS & SUPPLIERS

Spices

Green Saffron Spices

Unit 16, Knockgriffin,
Midleton, Cork, Ireland

Tel 00 353 21 463 7960

www.greensaffron.com

Arun and Olive Kapil's family business imports
and grinds premium spices from family farms
across India.

Fish

Ben's Fish

Rewsalls Old Barn, Rewsalls Lane,
East Mersea, Colchester,
Essex CO5 8SX

Tel 01206 386 833

www.bensfishmersea.co.uk

This supplier of fresh, seasonal fish and game is run
by Ben Woodcraft, who was an inshore fisherman for
20 years and now liases directly with local fishermen,
farmers and growers from around the east coast. Ben's
Fish is also a good supplier of English quinces.

Fish for Thought

The Cornish Fish Store, Unit 1,
Callywith Gate Business Park,
Launceston Road, Bodmin, Cornwall PL31 2RQ

Tel: 01208 262 202

www.fishforthought.org.uk

Fish for Thought send the freshest fish and seafood
straight from the Cornish seas to your front door. They
are the first online retailer to achieve MSC Accreditation,
and their boat, The Resolute, is recognised by the
Responsible Fishing Scheme. Fish can be requested
whole, headed and gutted, filleted or portioned, and
there's even a kids' box with skinned, pinned and de-
boned portions.

Graig Farm

Dolau, Llandrindod Wells,
Powys LD1 5TL

Tel: 01686 627 979

www.graigfarm.co.uk

This farm supplies a wide range of organic products,
including fish, meat and poultry, from its online shop.
All of their produce is cared for to high standards.

The Ethical Shellfish Company

Aros Mains, Isle of Mull,
Argyll PA72 6JP

Tel: 0845 116 2248

www.ethicalshellfishcompany.co.uk

Husband and wife team Guy and Juliet Grieve
established the Ethical Shellfish Company in April 2010
from their home on the Isle of Mull. As well as hand-
diving for scallops from their own boat in the Hebrides,
they buy sustainable shellfish from other fishermen,
ensuring that the king scallops, lobster, langoustine and
edible crab they sell is creel-caught, hand-fished, hand-
gathered, hand-dived, or line caught – and therefore your
dinner is 100 per cent ethically sound.

Wingham's Fresh Fish

108 Queen Street, Withernsea,
East Yorkshire HU19 2HB

Tel 01964 614 239

Shaun Wingham is one of a small number of license
holders permitted to catch Wild Salmon, Sea Trout and
MSC certified wild Sea Bass from the Holderness Coast
fishery – one of the most sustainably managed in the UK.
His wife Penny manages the shop, which is well worth
a visit.

Young's

www.youngsseafood.co.uk

The UK's leading frozen fish brand, Young's supply
supermarkets with a great deal of cod and haddock,
but also 60 alternative species of fish: both wild-caught
and farmed. The company's award-winning Fish for
Life programme, initiated in 2006, helps to ensure
that the everyday fish we eat is sustainable, with
every purchasing decision being made with a clear
understanding of the capacity of the environment to
support the fishing or fish farming effort involved.

Equipment

Lakeland

Alexandra Buildings, Windermere,
Cumbria LA23 1BQ

Tel 015394 88100

www.lakeland.co.uk

Lakeland provides an array of innovative cookware, appliances and utensils. The company places enormous value on customer satisfaction, and uses customer feedback to develop its vast range.

Nisbets Catering Equipment

Fourth Way, Avonmouth,
Bristol BS11 8TB

Tel 0845 140 5555

www.nisbets.co.uk

This is one of the UK's largest suppliers of catering equipment, and a great source of larger scale cooking equipment such as stock pots.

Useful organisations

The British Association for Shooting and Conservation

Marford Mill, Rossett,
Wrexham, LL12 0HL

Tel 01244 573 000

www.basc.org.uk

BASC promote and protect sporting shooting of all types throughout the UK, and produce Codes of Practice detailing the law surrounding shooting game.

FARMA

Lower Ground Floor, 12 Southgate Street,
Winchester, Hampshire SO23 9EF

Tel 0845 458 8420

www.farmersmarkets.net

The National Farmers' Retail & Markets Association represents the sale of local food and fresh farm products direct to the public through farmers' markets and farm shops. Visit their website for a list of certified markets and suppliers in your area.

Freedom Food Limited

Wilberforce Way,
Southwater, Horsham,
West Sussex RH139RS

Tel 0300 123 0014

www.rspca.org.uk/freedomfood

Freedom Food is the RSPCA's farm assurance and food labelling scheme. It is the only UK farm assurance scheme to focus solely on improving the welfare of farm animals reared for food.

Marine Stewardship Council

Marine House, 1 Snow Hill,
London EC1A 2DH

Tel 020 7246 8900

www.msc.org

The Marine Stewardship Council fishery certification program and seafood ecolabel recognise and reward sustainable fishing. This global organisation works with fisheries, seafood companies, scientists, conservation groups and the public to promote the best environmental choices in seafood.

Slow Food UK

Slow Food UK, 6 Neal's Yard,
Covent Garden,
London WC2H 9DP

Tel 020 7099 1132

www.slowfood.org.uk

Slow Food UK is part of the global Slow Food movement. It has thousands of members and connections with local groups around the UK that link the pleasure of artisan food to community and the environment.

GLOSSARY OF COOKING TERMS

Many languages have influenced the British kitchen, but none so much as French – hardly surprising since French food has often been held up as the benchmark for excellence, in Mrs Beeton's time as well as in our own. Long before the Michelin guide began to report on British restaurants, French chefs were working for British royalty and could be found in the kitchens of many large country houses. Perhaps the most famous of these was Antonin Carême, chef to the Prince Regent (later George IV), who set the standard for future chefs to emulate. Mrs Beeton knew of him by name and reputation. The list below is intended to help explain the more commonly used terms – many, but not all, of which come from the French.

au gratin describes a cooked dish topped with a browned crust, usually made by finishing with grated cheese or breadcrumbs and browning under the grill

bain marie a large pan or tin used as a waterbath to cook or warm food that is too delicate to withstand direct heat

beat to mix food energetically to introduce air, using a wooden spoon, whisk or electric mixer to make a mixture light and fluffy

beurre manie a paste made from butter and flour that is used to thicken hot sauces

beurre noisette butter heated until it has coloured to a rich brown, then mixed with vinegar or lemon juice and, often, capers

bisque a shellfish stock or soup, often with added cream

blanch to boil briefly, often in order to loosen the skin from nuts and kernels, to part-cook green vegetables or to remove strong or bitter flavours

bone to remove the bones from fish, meat or poultry

braise to cook slowly in a covered pan or dish, with liquid

brine a saltwater solution used for preserving and pickling

brown to colour the surface of a food by cooking it in hot fat, caramelising the sugars and developing flavour

chinois a conical sieve with a very fine mesh used for straining soups, sauces and purées to give a very smooth result

clarify (of stock) to remove sediment or filter using egg white

clarified butter pure butterfat, made by heating butter and lifting the fat from the liquid milk that forms underneath. Clarified butter does not burn as easily as butter and has a longer shelf life

coral (of lobster) the ovaries and preformed eggs of a hen lobster, found in the tail; (of scallops) the orange roe, which is often detached before cooking

court bouillon a stock flavoured with herbs and vegetables, to be used for poaching fish

cure to preserve fish or meat by salting, smoking or drying

de-glaze to add liquid to a pan after roasting or sautéeing in order to dissolve any juices or sediment left in the base of the pan, picking up their flavour

dress to prepare poultry, game or shellfish

emulsion a suspension of tiny droplets of one liquid in another liquid

flake to separate the flesh of fish into small pieces following the natural structure

flambé or flame to remove the alcohol from hot food by lighting the fumes

liaison a thickening or binding agent, for example a roux, arrowroot mixture, egg yolk or cream

maître d'hôtel cooked and/or served with parsley

mirepoix a mixture of finely chopped vegetables, usually onion, carrot and celery

par-boil   to part cook in water

pickle   to preserve meat, fish or vegetables in brine or vinegar

poach   to cook food in simmering liquid

preserve   to keep food in good condition by treating it with salt, vinegar or sugar

reduce   to concentrate a liquid, for example a sauce or stock, by boiling it until a portion has evaporated

score   to cut shallow gashes into the surface of food before cooking

seasoned flour   flour mixed with salt and pepper, and sometimes other spices, often used to coat meat or fish before cooking

season   to add salt, pepper, spices, herbs or other ingredients to food to add flavour or (at the end of the cooking time) to correct the balance of flavours

skillet   a heavy cast iron frying pan

soused   pickled in brine or vinegar

steam   to cook food in the steam that rises from a pan of boiling water

strain   to separate liquids from solids by passing through a sieve or muslin

sweat   to gently soften chopped vegetables in hot oil or butter

vinaigrette   a dressing for salad or vegetables, made with base of oil and vinegar

whip   to beat eggs or cream until they are thick and increased in volume

INDEX

ACKNOWLEDGEMENTS

Mum, Sandra Baker, helped without question in the kitchen and office both in the process of testing the recipes and in organising manuscripts – you are a blessing. To my sister Louise, and to Oscar and Fanny for providing moral support go hearty thanks.

Much respect and love goes to Dad, John Baker, for taking me fishing to Spurn Head where I caught my first Dabs.

My cousin Shaun Wingham and his wife Penny have been hugely supportive and influential in their willingness to jump into the sea at all times of day and night to provide fish for my kitchen.

Had I not worked with Joyce Molyneux, I would probably never have known the joys of Mediterranean fish cookery. She is a delight and a true friend.

Adam Sellar provided great support in the kitchen during the testing of the recipes – thank you.

Amanda Harris and Debbie Woska sat through the creation of *Mrs Beeton How to Cook* with me – providing just the right amount of support and encouragement – thank you.

Zelda Turner and Damian Currie deserve thanks for helping trim and sculpt the recipes in this smaller collection.

To all the design team – Julyan Bayes, Lucie Steriker, Sammy-Jo Squire and her crew, and the photographer Andrew Hayes-Watkins and his team for making the book look so beautiful.

The team behind the scenes at Orion helped enormously – Elizabeth Allen and Nicky Carswell especially.

Thanks to the Marine Stewardship Council for their guide to buying fish in season.

Finally, thanks to all of the lifeboat men and their families who continue to work in the worst possible conditions to keep an eye on all of us who enjoy the waves.

Gerard Baker